BOOK ^{OF} _{THE} DEAD

Bob Weir & Otis.

BOOK OF THE DEAD

Celebrating 25 Years with the Grateful Dead

Photographs by Herb Greene
Foreword by Robert Hunter

Delacorte Press
Delta

Ron "Pigpen" McKernan
September 8, 1945/March 8, 1973

Delacorte Press and Delta Books
Published by
Dell Publishing
a division of
Bantam Doubleday Dell Publishing Group, Inc.
666 Fifth Avenue
New York, New York 10103

Book and cover design: Ingalls + Associates, San
Francisco
Designers: Gail Grant, Thomas Ingalls
Composition: MasterType, San Francisco
On Line Typography, San Francisco
Prints: Spindler Photographic Services

Library of Congress Cataloging in Publication Data

Greene, Herb, 1942–
    Book of the Dead

1. Grateful Dead (Musical group)—Pictorial works.
2. Rock Musicians—United States—Pictorial works.
I. Title.
ML421.G72G73 1990 782.42166'092'2
89-23716 (hc)
89-23717 (pbk)
ISBN 0-385-30088-3 (hc)
ISBN 0-385-29947-8 (pbk)

Printed in the United States of America
Published Simultaneously in Canada

April 1990

10   9   8   7   6   5   4   3   2

CONTENTS

Robert Hunter, Lyricist, Grateful Dead.

FOREWORD

When Herb Greene asked me to write a foreword to this book I protested that I knew nothing about photography beyond the mechanics of the pinhole camera. Herb replied: "Just tell the truth about what went down — if you dare!" Well, I don't take a dare lightly and besides he wasn't asking for anything physically strenuous. The truth? Sure — that's easy. Er... Once upon a time — no, let's see now — ah!... A furious storm raged and the arms of the tree on the terrace dripped thick black drops like nearly coagulated blood upon the...

Look — a lot of this has happened before. The hydraulic pressure of a generational cycle molding new kinds of creatures out of the common pool of parts. First there's a kind of lull when it seems nothing's happening — it's more or less dark everywhere. You go down to the cellar thinking a fuse needs changing. After a bit of kicking around in the dark you realize it's not a blown fuse at all — it's the cellar that needs replacing — at which point it is no longer dark but about a quarter century into another round of misconstrued daylight. Don't say too much about it — *it never made sense and it never will.* Whatever you decide can only be an example of your peculiar cultural perspective.

I've read a lot about the Grateful Dead in the last quarter century and never felt much of it was near the mark. Yet testimony helps create a perception of what it was seen to be which influences what it is, since, transactional by nature, it cannot be separated from reflections of itself, however skewed. My own objectivity is hopelessly determined by my involvement as a co-creator. The actual factors involved are too multifarious to expect a satisfying reduction.

What does seem to be true is that there is a powerful resonance in the juxtaposition of the words: *Grateful Dead.* Once heard, the name is not forgotten. Had it been *Cruel Potato*, we might have a different situation to extrapolate — or none at all.

Perhaps the key to the Dead's latter-day "success" involved keeping the act together through various scenarios until it grew *into* that ominous name, originally many sizes too big for those who chose it, or who were chosen by or *because of it*. A bond of mutually reinforced identity evolved which was separate neither from the logo nor its particular embodiment.

I won't speak here of the Dead's specific contributions to Americana, or of the personalities involved, only of their received role as *cultural icon*, which I feel beclouds consideration of their actual achievements in widening the *scope* of popular music. They probably encompass as many categories within their repertoire as the rest of currently popular music does within its total genre. Not a distinction calculated to push a lot of product to a public with fixed expectations of what is acceptable over a car speaker.

The flamboyance of the name brought challenge. GRATEFUL DEAD BUSTED brought headlines which LOVELORN COW-BOYS ARRESTED might have failed to do. The name had built-in nuisance value betokening unspeakable attitudes. It became a sine qua non for the supposed chasm between generations and seemed to promise anarchy, non-dialectical immaterialism and a general war on niceness. It was...*A Teddy Bear from Hell!* If the musical evidence generally contradicts this, the image made good copy and the onus stuck. So far as I know, whether innocently mythologized or overtly deconstructed, the Grateful Dead have always been subjected to critical treatment with reference to a self-manufacturing extrinsic iconology. What lies beneath the bones?

Does anyone think the Dead *made it* because of good looks, impeccable musicianship or blockbuster material? Look at the photos, listen to the records, observe that the first "hit" didn't occur until the late '80s, almost as an afterthought.

Could it be that the name itself was responsible? A name is a handle; a handle is a lever — give it a fulcrum (to the '60s) and make it long enough, extended to the dawn of the '90s — and it might indeed move exceptional weights should it observe a few non-obvious rules. Above all, *don't direct it*. Let it kinda...*run itself*. Stay in solution until something precipitates. Don't tag it with assigned or imagined values but let it descend into the form which best expresses it. Don't confuse it with individuals or a certain style. It accrues these, but that isn't its essential nature, although it can only be apprehended by means of its expressions.

This point of view subtracts nothing from the credit due the talents instrumental in the arousal and implementation of the phenomenon. It just tones down the insupportable shine resulting from identification of human agency with the transformational capacity of a potent symbol, with results often incapacitating to the agent, and puts the onus on the logos.

Which is where the pictures come in. Photos present iconography on a different scale than words and music: a scale of light and angle rather than sound and speech. When Herb Greene adjusts the lighting *just so*, powders out some glare and revamps the contrast in the darkroom, he is participating in mythmaking: imbuing the criteria with meaningfulness — though it is improbable that he thinks of his task in these terms. He is only producing the best photograph his skills allow. Gainsay what the precise meaning of the work might be, it is the *immanence* of such meaning which separates a photograph from a snapshot; the intention of the eye behind the shutter to satisfy the demands of signifying composition and the ability to recognize when the elements coalesce. Herb has always been among the best at inventing these moments.

Getting back to the initial dare, all I can truthfully say is that, like Kilroy, the *Grateful Dead* were here. It doesn't make sense in any conventional way, but it *does* signify. It was a joy and a caution to be near the center of such a phenomenon in the full rapture of its blooming. Here are some of its petals preserved in a solution of silver nitrate by a gentleman with a respectable eye for the inherent strangeness of it.

ROBERT HUNTER
August 1989

ACKNOWLEDGMENTS

Who is responsible for this? I won't take all the blame. A few crucial culprits helped me with this project in one way or another. David and Sissy Spindler expertly printed the images. Gail Grant and Tom Ingalls did a pretty darn good job of designing the whole thing. Bob Miller and Tony Secunda let the deal go down. Robert Hunter and David Gans contributed kind words.

Way, way back in the Sixties, certain people (you know who you are) supported and understood what I was trying to capture. I'd like to thank them all. Line up in alphabetical order. Most of all, I'm beholden to Gene and Sara Estribou, who graciously shared their home with my darkroom. I'm thankful for Maruska Nelson's enduring patience and for our beautiful daughter, Eden.

My wife Ilze, a most reluctant Deadhead, has my gratitude for her steadfast encouragement and love and for a brand-new Deadhead, our daughter Charlotte Rose.

And of course, thanks go to the boys in the band for doing whatever it is they've been doing for the last twenty-five years. Without them, this book would be a never was and I'd be an insurance salesman.

HERB GREENE
San Francisco
August 1989

WARLOCKS

1965

Warlocks, 1965. Jerry Garcia, Bill Kreutzmann, Bob Weir,
Phil Lesh & Ron "Pigpen" McKernan.

BOOK OF THE DEAD

GRATEFUL DEAD
HAIGHT ASHBURY

1966

Grateful Dead, 1966. Jerry Garcia, Ron "Pigpen" McKernan,
Phil Lesh, Bob Weir & Bill Kreutzmann.

Grateful Dead with Jack Casady (Jefferson Airplane).

GRATEFUL DEAD
710 ASHBURY

1966

*Grateful Dead, 1966. Bill Kreutzmann, Ron ''Pigpen''
McKernan, Phil Lesh, Jerry Garcia & Bob Weir.*

44

Danny Rifkin.

Ron "Pigpen" McKernan, Tangerine, Jerry Garcia,
Phil Lesh, Rosie, Laird, Bill Kreutzmann, Bob Weir,
Danny Rifkin & Rock Scully.

Drivin' That Train

1966

Grateful Dead, 1966. Bob Weir, Phil Lesh, Ron "Pigpen" McKernan, Bill Kreutzmann & Jerry Garcia.

54

Rancho Olompali
Marin County

1966

Jack Casady, Jefferson Airplane.

Dan Hicks, Charlatans.

Peter Albin, Big Brother & the Holding Company.

Darby Slick, The Great Society.

Grace Slick, The Great Society.

Neal Cassady.

Ben Van Meter, Avalon Light Show.

Alton Kelley, poster artist.

Ron Thelin, The Psychedelic Shop.

Chet Helms, Avalon Ballroom.

George Hunter, Charlatans.

Jerry Garcia & Jerry Slick, The Great Society.

78

GRATEFUL DEAD
HAIGHT STREET

1967-1968

Grateful Dead, 1967. Phil Lesh, Bill Kreutzmann, Bob Weir,
Ron "Pigpen" McKernan & Jerry Garcia.

Mickey Hart.

Susila & Bill Kreutzmann.

88

Mountain Girl.

Baker Street, San Francisco

1967

Danny Rifkin & Rock Scully.

GRATEFUL DEAD, LAGUNA STREET

1969

Grateful Dead, 1969. Tom "TC" Constanten, Bob Weir, Bill Kreutzmann, Ron "Pigpen" McKernan, Phil Lesh, Mickey Hart & Jerry Garcia.

112

Grateful Dead & David "Rickey" Nelson, John "Marmaduke" Dawson, New Riders of the Purple Sage.

SHOW ME SOMETHING BUILT TO LAST

Most of us Deadheads are Kennedy kids. Jerry Garcia is our big brother and Jack Kerouac is our black-sheep uncle. We white, suburban, American, born-in-the-'50s children of professionals were treated to a deliriously upbeat set of values and opportunities; this was America at its most confident, generous and tolerant. Free of misery and oppression, we came of age listening to the rich and playful music of the Beatles and the others illuminated by their genius. At the end of *Yellow Submarine*, as the smoke cleared following the defeat of the Blue Meanies, the horizon was filled with letters a mile high spelling out YES. That was the sixties.

It is a fascinating irony, now that we are expected to just say "no," that the punch was first spiked by Uncle Sam himself: LSD was introduced into the community by government cold-warriors in mind-control experiments at a local Veterans Administration hospital. For novelist Ken Kesey, musician/poet Robert Hunter, and others who were paid to take the drug, LSD opened the door to the immense vistas of truth and fun inside our skulls.

And they brought some home to share with their friends. The powerful psychedelic was the social and creative lubricant in a series of multimedia parties staged by Kesey's band of Merry Pranksters and attended by the Grateful Dead, functioning not as performers but rather as one of many unconstrained participants in the intentional chaos. Long nights in neighborhood bars had given them repertoire and endurance; the Acid Tests gave them *license*. LSD was the crucible in which Jerry Garcia, Phil Lesh, Bob Weir, Bill Kreutzmann and Mickey Hart (Ron "Pigpen" McKernan, their R&B-singing front man, never indulged in psychedelics) alloyed their talents and their influences to frame the unique musical language they have continued to expand and refine over the years.

The government set the stage for the counterculture when, by fiat, it made criminals of the civilian scientists who continued the experiment outside the VA hospital. Owsley Stanley, justly legendary for the quality of his product and what would later come to be known as "market penetration," used the Dead as a proving ground for his labors in both chemistry and audio. He built a sound system with some of the income from his mission, and he supported and recorded the Grateful Dead while they developed their unique and ambitious musical language.

Then the Dead moved into San Francisco, where the musicians took great sustenance from the wildly eclectic scene that flowered in a neighborhood near San Francisco State College. Photographer Herbie Greene, who hung out with Mike Ferguson of the seminal Haight-Ashbury band The Charlatans, loved the music and began to take pictures of the bands. "I was the long-haired guy with the camera," Greene recalls. "All the guys with the guitars became the bands, and I was serious about photography so I became the photographer." As the scene developed, so did Greene's professional stature. He shot the cover of Jefferson Airplane's *Surrealistic Pillow* and provided the band shots used by Alton Kelley in his collage for the cover of the Grateful Dead's first album.

The music business harvested some of those acts and ate the rest alive. The ballrooms nurtured native talent, and "dance hall keeper" Bill Graham brought in a magnificent selection of musicians to entertain and inspire the locals who shared those stages. But the ballroom scene became a casualty of the music's popularity, and when the record business took over — on its terms — many practitioners of the "San Francisco Sound" had a hard time assimilating into the increasingly rigid stylistic strata defined by radio.

The Grateful Dead, able to deliver a whole lot of stuff but rarely vanilla on demand, fell out of favor with album-rock radio pretty early on; and they couldn't even crash the parking lot of the Top Forty. But they connected with an audience that appreciated their earthy experimentalism and has continued to support the band for twenty-five years of pluralistic, non-hierarchical, collective creation.

The Grateful Dead are not the only Sixties survivor extant, but they are an extraordinarily successful one in both economic and creative terms. They were a band like many other bands until LSD came along and upped the creative ante. Acid had a powerful direct and indirect influence on the arts and letters of the mid-'60s; through LSD, consciousness became a playground and a field of endeavor. And when the drug faded from the scene the Grateful Dead continued to develop a musical framework impervious to shifting trends and challenging enough to sustain the interest of the musicians and their audience through the ensuing decades.

The Grateful Dead have always been able to concentrate on the spontaneous creation of music rather than the rote performance of carefully planned sets. The rest of rock now concentrates on polished, precise presentations, while the Dead remain free to follow their collective instinct out at the edge of their continually expanding musical landscape.

The Dead's commercial solipsism has infuriated some critics over the years. It was their unruliness that rankled the industry at first, and then it was their inconsistency. In the '80s, having settled in to life as a touring ensemble (they continued to make records, with varying degrees of satisfaction and no appreciable chart impact until 1987's *In the Dark*), they encountered the nervous hostility of rock critics who went off half-cocked over the Dead's blithe disregard for the dictates of the marketing establishment — but no one cocks an eyebrow at a baseball fan who takes in an entire home stand, so let's just say the Dead are more like the Chicago Cubs than a rock band and leave it at that.

The continuity of our fandom more closely resembles that of baseball than of rock. Bill Graham notes, for example, that while heavy metal fans move on to other styles as the ravages of puberty ease off, Deadheads stay with the band through college and on into adulthood. I know several families with three generations of Deadheads who all attend concerts together — again, more like baseball than rock 'n' roll.

The lineup is more stable than that of a baseball team, though. The Grateful Dead is an art commune that made it. They don't live together anymore, but they work together with the intimacy of the Wallendas and the polymorphous synchrony of a baseball team (and thank God it's not vice versa!). All they wanted in the first place was the freedom to (excuse the expression) "do their own thing," and at that they have succeeded enviably. A subculture has formed around the Grateful Dead with sufficient weight to sustain the band's pursuit of its collective instinct, and although the band has long since given up any attempt to swing the world over to their way of thinking, they do offer an example of *right livelihood* that has inspired many people to take career paths designed to keep their lives interesting and meaningful. "We're just doing what can be done," says Jerry Garcia.

The Dead as a social and economic entity represent a greater degree of individual expression and responsibility than the typical American worker ever sees. The anarchy of the band's musical interaction (and remember, "anarchy" means an absence of rulers, not an absence of rules) is reflected in uncircumscribed jobs that would be hard to describe on an organization chart. "We're living our life through this medium, 'Grateful Deadness'–whatever that is," says Garcia. "We definitely want it to have as much room as it can possibly have, and that means it should be able to incorporate all the shading and all the changes that you can possibly put yourself through. It should have that much room — otherwise we would be making it too small."

The diffusion of authority is one of the most important aspects of the Grateful Dead paradigm: although Jerry Garcia is the most incandescent character in this corner of the galaxy, it is by no means a Hieronymocentric system.

Bob Weir characterizes the band as "a bunch of guys who would probably amount to neighborhood heroes but for the fact that they've fallen in with each other." Their innate understanding of each other and their concerted sense of quest coaxes out of them what on a good night I would equate with genius. I've seen what satisfies my criteria for genius displayed by the various members of the group, almost always in response to a stimulus offered by someone else in the group.

"The most I've ever amounted to is through concerted effort with other people," Weir continues. "The better I can do for them, the better they'll do for me." It is a musical marriage, historically noteworthy for its longevity and the quantity and quality of its output.

What the Grateful Dead have achieved is simple and all-encompassing in its importance: job security. Their failure to penetrate the record charts and radio playlists has worked to their advantage by allowing them to escape the creative tradeoffs that bedevil those whose careers depend on the shifting winds of popular merchandising.

In a sense, the "American dream" — the promised reward for years of backbreaking work and devotion to the Company — comes down to the freedom to dress casually and sleep late on weekdays. And the Grateful Dead have that now.

So when you look at these pictures, you are looking at some satisfied specimens. "For me, the idea of being able to make a living at playing music is so delightful," Garcia said in a 1981 interview. "Before the Grateful Dead, I spent most of my time supporting my music habit. It's just amazingly lucky to be able to do something in this life that makes people happy."

DAVID GANS
August 1989

GRATEFUL DEAD

1979

Grateful Dead, 1979. Jerry Garcia, Bob Weir, Phil Lesh,
Bill Kreutzmann, Mickey Hart & Brent Mydland.

IN THE DARK • DYLAN/DEAD

1987

Grateful Dead, 1987. Bob Weir, Jerry Garcia, Mickey Hart,
Bill Kreutzmann, Phil Lesh & Brent Mydland.

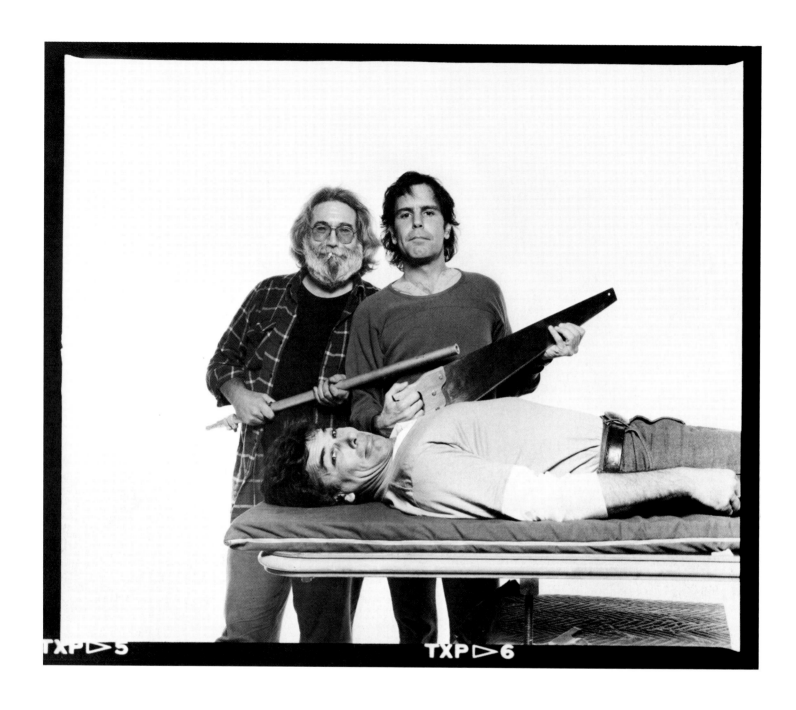

TXP▷5   TXP▷6

146

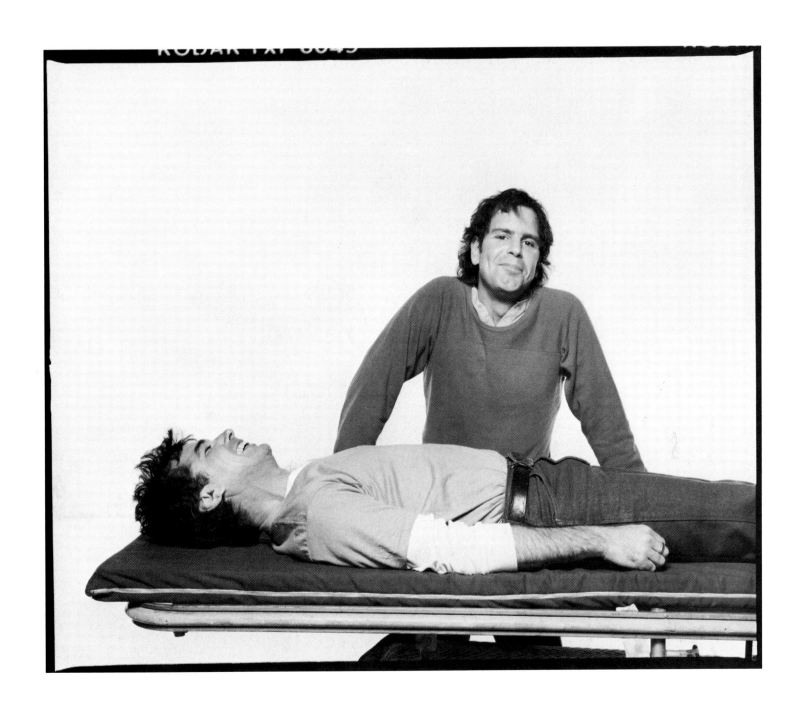

Jon McIntire, Manager, Grateful Dead
& Bob Weir.

John Cutler, Producer, Grateful Dead & Mickey Hart.

150

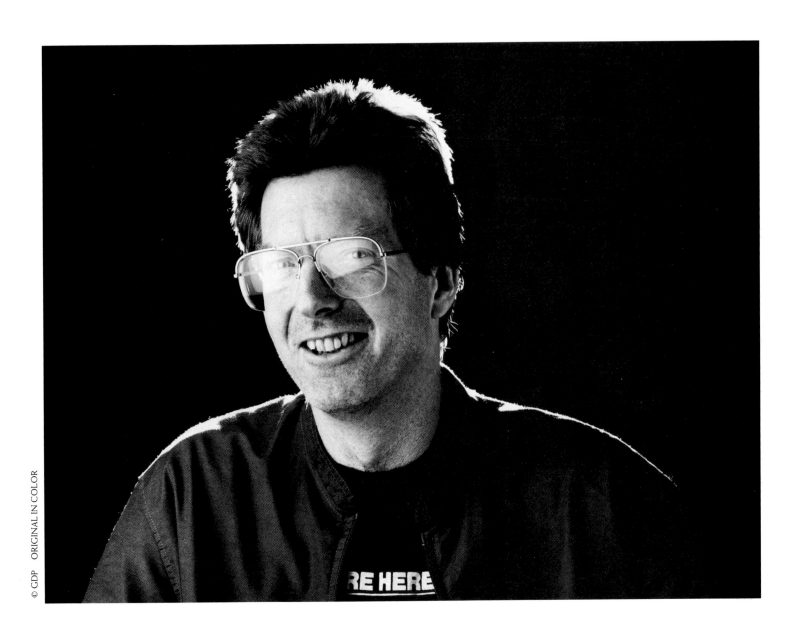

Garcia on Broadway.

154

The Crew.

IMMORTALITY AT REASONABLE RATES

H·B·GREENE·

·SAN FRANCISCO·

LIMITED EDITION PHOTOGRAPHS
AVAILABLE FROM
ROBERT KOCH GALLERY, SAN FRANCISCO